Practical Guide to Emotional Intelligence Mastery 2.0

How to Read Emotions, Analyze People, and Influence Anyone with Body Language, Mind Control, NLP, Persuasion, and Manipulation Techniques

Written by Daniel James

Practical Guide to Emotional Intelligence Mastery 2.0
© **Copyright 2018 by Gary Ramsey - All rights reserved.**

The following eBook is reproduced below with the goal of providing information that is as accurate and reliable as possible. Regardless, purchasing this eBook can be seen as consent to the fact that both the publisher and the author of this book are in no way experts on the topics discussed within and that any recommendations or suggestions that are made herein are for entertainment purposes only. Professionals should be consulted as needed prior to undertaking any of the action endorsed herein.

This declaration is deemed fair and valid by both the American Bar Association and the Committee of Publishers Association and is legally binding throughout the United States.

Furthermore, the transmission, duplication or reproduction of any of the following work including specific information will be considered an illegal act irrespective of if it is done electronically or in print. This extends to creating a secondary or tertiary copy of the work or a recorded copy and is only allowed with an expressed written consent from the Publisher. All additional rights reserved.

The information in the following pages is broadly considered to be a truthful and accurate account of facts and as such any inattention, use or misuse of the information in question by the reader will render any resulting actions solely under their purview. There are no scenarios in which the publisher or the original author of this work can be in any fashion deemed liable for any hardship or damages that may befall them after undertaking information described herein.

Additionally, the information in the following pages is intended only for informational purposes and should thus be thought of as universal. As befitting its nature, it is presented without assurance regarding its prolonged validity or interim quality. Trademarks that are mentioned are done without written consent and can in no way be considered an endorsement from the trademark holder.

Daniel James
Table of Contents

Introduction..6

Chapter 1: How to Read Emotions......................9

Chapter 2: How to Analyze People....................31

Chapter 3: Persuasion Techniques....................47

Chapter 4: Manipulation Techniques................75

Chapter 5: Body Language Techniques.............89

Chapter 6: Mind Control Techniques...............119

Chapter 7: NLP Methods..................................142

Conclusion..163

Introduction

Congratulations on downloading *Practical Guide to Emotional Intelligence Mastery 2.0* and thank you for doing so.

The following chapters will discuss how you can further develop your emotional intelligence and use it in order to influence anyone. These tips can help you influence anyone from your neighbor to your best friend or a family member or even someone you just met.

Have you ever wondered what it would be like to influence people to act a certain way? Would you like to finally be able to get that raise from work? Would you like to be able to get a friend or a family member to do favors for you, in a way that makes them feel like they are benefiting? Are you interested in learning how to work with manipulation, mind control, persuasion, and NLP techniques? If this sounds like you, then this is the guidebook you need to look through.

In this guidebook, we will look at a variety of techniques that you can use to do this influencing. The method you choose may depend on what you want to get out of the situation and who you are working with. In any case, your emotional intelligence can help because this allows you to better understand the emotions of the other person, and to control your own emotions as well. Once you have mastered this skill, various influencing techniques like mind control, persuasion, NLP, and even your body language can be yours to use.

When you are ready to use your emotional intelligence to get more of what you want out of life, take a look through this guidebook and see what you can learn!

There are plenty of books on this subject on the market, thanks again for choosing this one! Every effort was made to ensure it is full of as much useful information as possible, please enjoy!

Daniel James
Chapter 1: How to Read Emotions

One skill that can really help you get ahead in your career and in your personal life is the ability to read emotions and figure out what the other person feels or means by something, even if the words don't say it. There are times when someone is sad or mad or upset, but the words they tell you to say the exact opposite. Being able to look at body language and other nonverbal cues can make a difference on how well you understand the other person. But being able to read emotions can be tough.

Most of us grew up being able to understand language and the words others are telling us in a conversation. Some, but not all, also learned how to read nonverbal cues to see what the real meaning is behind the words. Some people are really good at doing this, and others will struggle a little bit.

The thing about language is that humans are able to communicate through many different avenues. They can use their words, the tone or the sound of their voice, their hand gestures, their body language, and even their facial expressions to help them communicate properly. Sometimes this happens even without them having full control over it. Being able to recognize these signs will take you a long way in recognizing the emotions that the other person has.

The ability you have to read and then respond to emotions as you see them in others is known as emotional intelligence. When you work to develop this emotional intelligence, you can then improve awareness of the emotion, not only in others but also in yourself. That is why this chapter will take time to help you learn the best tricks when it is time to read emotions in other people and in yourself.

Daniel James
How to Analyze the Emotions in Others

The first thing we will explore is how to recognize both negative and positive emotions in the other person. There are many different types of emotions, but they will often fall into one of two categories, either positive emotions or negative ones. While these emotions can all be different, they do have some similarities and actions that come together and help them be associated with each other. These similarities include:

Positive emotions: When someone is experiencing a positive emotion, they will have reduced levels of stress, a better mood, and their awareness and memory will be better. These would include such emotions like inspiration, relief, confidence, love, sympathy, surprise, and happiness.

Negative emotions: When someone is experiencing negative emotions, they will have stress levels that are higher. They will also be able to recognize threats better and may be able to use these in order to deal with any situation that seems challenging. Some examples of this emotion would include disgust, anger, contempt, sadness, and fear.

While these two categories of emotions are pretty easy to understand, the big question is how you will be able to recognize them in the person you are communicating with. The answer is to look towards the mouth and the eyes. In general, many emotions are going to be expressed through both the mouth and the eyes. The region of the face where the emotions are most likely to show up will be influenced more by culture. For example, if you are talking to someone from Japan, you would want to look more towards the eyes to tell emotion. In Europe and the United States, you will see more emotion near the mouth.

The best thing to do is look at the whole face, rather than the eyes, to tell what the emotion is. If it still seems to be hard to find, then you can look at each of the areas to see what happens. When observing the face for emotions, stand a few feet away from the other person. This allows you to still carry on a normal conversation, but you are far away enough that you can look over their whole face.

You should also take note of the tone of voice that someone is using during the conversation to figure out what they are feeling. People can often use their voices to help show their emotions, and as a way to control their emotions. This works well for some emotions like anger or sadness, but for others, such as contentment, stress, or boredom, the tone of voice may not be able to tell you as much. In addition, some voice tones are going to work for several emotions at once, so you really need to pay attention to some of the other signs, such as the facial expression, to help you out.

Next, it is a good idea to note the general behavior of the other person. If you look at that person, do they portray a friendly atmosphere back to you, or do they seem more reserved when talking? Emotions can be experienced in a manner that makes the other person unconscious of what is going on. Using your best judgment and following that gut feeling will sometimes be enough to help you read an emotion, even when none of the other signs are working.

Often, being able to recognize the emotion that is going on with others can become easier when you note the way that you react to the other person. Often, you will find that you will mirror the emotions of others in terms of your behavior, tone of voice, and expression. If you are talking to someone who is sad, for example, you may unconsciously start to mirror them and show symptoms of being ad as well.

Another thing to look at is the physical well-being of the other person. It is possible that the emotions of that person could influence their health. This goes both ways. If the person is generally happy and shows a lot of excitement, this can influence their health for the better. But, if that person is often angry or sad or depressed, this could end up harming their health.

With those negative emotions, there are a lot of physical symptoms that can show up. The person may end up with low energy, problems in their stomach, changes in their eating habits, and migraines. Signs of mental illness or depression could include things like confusion, isolation from those they care about, and unable to cope with some common problems.

The best thing you can do here is to learn how to develop and then improve your emotional intelligence. You can do this by teaching yourself the best ways to recognize the emotions that others are feeling and then also learn how to become more aware of the emotions that you deal with. How are you supposed to be able to recognize emotions in others and help them out if you have no idea how to handle these emotions in your own life?

Remember that there are four branches that come with emotional intelligence. These include being able to recognize emotions as they come in yourself and those around you, being able to use those emotions to promote thinking, understanding the significance of all the emotions, and how to manage those emotions. Some of the strategies that you can try to help improve your emotional intelligence include:

- Get away from the technology: Make sure to turn that phone off and step away from the computer. Spend more time with face to face communication of those around you, rather than looking at a screen and hoping to get some connection. Have these conversations with others on a daily basis.
- Don't back away when there is an emotion or a feeling that is uncomfortable for

others or for yourself. These may not be fun to deal with, but they are necessary. Instead of running from the situation, take some time and think what the reason is that you feel this way. Then after you are done recognizing that emotion, try to counteract it by coming up with three positive emotions to replace it.

- Listen to what your body is saying: Your gut can often catch on to things long before you do. If you feel that your heart is fluttering or your stomach is in a knot, there is probably something going on and you should listen.

- Keep a journal or some kind of record about the thoughts that you have. Then, once a week or once a month, go through and read those thoughts and see what you can do to improve them and what you are doing well with at the time.

Practical Guide to Emotional Intelligence Mastery 2.0
Interpreting Facial Expressions

The face can give out a lot of information about a person. It is really hard for most people to hide their emotions from their face. They may try to smile and say the right things, but the eyes, or the mouth, or something else can often give them away. If you are trying to read the emotions of another person, then this is the place for you to start.

First, you must take a look at the facial expressions of the other person. The emotions that people are feeling inside will be expressed on their faces and in the eyes. Being able to recognize the association that occurs between certain types of emotions and their corresponding facial expressions can help you complete this task.

Remember not to be fooled here. Sometimes people are really good at manipulating their facial expressions. Often they will do this to try and appear happy when they are really sad or angry. They may not want you to know how they are feeling or they just don't want to draw attention to themselves. This is why you should always look at more than one cue when reading emotions. Making eye contact and noting the tone of voice and other parts of the body language can really help.

As you get better at reading people and looking for emotions, you will be able to recognize a genuine smile. This kind of smile is going to use up more of the muscles in the face compared to one that is fake or forced. In a genuine smile, the corners of the mouth will be raised up. If you see that there are some muscles around the eyes that are tight and small wrinkles are there around the corners of the eyes, then this is a genuine smile.

Sometimes the hardest emotion to read is sadness. This is because the target won't want to make it obvious to you and to others that they are feeling sad. They may not want others to know about the situation, they may feel guilty for feeling sad, or they just worry how you will judge them for that emotion. They will try to hide their sadness by trying to come off as happy with smiles and other cues when they are sad.

Genuine happiness, on the other hand, is hard to fake. The target may be able to smile and try to get the signs of happiness to appear, but since happiness is so hard to fake, there will still be some signs or cues to tell you whether the target is actually happy or not. Sadness, if you are looking for it, will be associated with frowning, raising the inner corners of the eyebrow, loose eyelids, and more.

You can even use some of these tips to help recognize disgust and anger in the other person. These two emotions are the ones that are often associated with one another and they are going to have facial expressions that are very similar. For example, any time that we are angry, annoyed, or disgusted; we are more likely to wrinkle up our noses.

There are a lot of reasons why someone is going to feel angry. They may be mad that things aren't going their way or that they aren't getting the results that they wanted. No matter the reason for feeling angry, you will notice some of the same signs. The eyebrows are going to be pulled down, the lips will be tight, and there will be a slight bulge in the eyes.

As a contrast to this anger, some other negative emotions like disgust, disdain, and dislike, will result in a raised upper lip while the lower lip is kind of loose. You will also pull the eyebrows down a bit, but this won't be as dramatic as it was during anger.

And finally, you can also read the emotions of surprise and fear on the targets face. While surprise is seen as more of a positive emotion and fear is more negative, both trigger the same part of the brain and will give you similar results with the target. When something happens that the target wasn't expecting, whether it is something good or something bad, then a part of the brain that we don't have control over will become stimulated. This results in a pulling up of the eyelids and eyebrows and the eyes will be nice and wide.

Fear will show up in the face with the eyebrows pulled in towards the nose and the pupils will dilate, or get bigger, to help take in light. The mouth will often be open as well. We will sometimes start to tense up the muscles of the face a bit, but this is most noticeable around the cheeks and the mouth. When it comes to feeling surprised, we are more likely to arch the eyebrows and then drop the jaw. The mouth will stay open with the muscles near it loose and relaxed during this time.

Other Ways to Read Emotions

Just by looking at the facial features of the other person, paying attention to the words they are saying, and listening to the different tones of voice they use, you will quickly start to notice the emotions that they are feeling. Even if the person is trying to keep an emotion from you, those who have higher levels of emotional intelligence will be able to catch even the subtle cues and can tell what emotion is actually there.

There are also a few other things that you can look for to better tell what emotions the other person is feeling. Nonverbal cues can really tell you a lot about the other person. They can sometimes be misleading, especially if you are new to trying it out because each person may respond differently. Either way, they are still really helpful when it comes to being able to read emotions in the other person.

The right nonverbal cues are going to help you to notice emotions through eye contact, body movements, and the posture. Making an effort to notice whether that target is animated in the story they are telling or do they seem tense and stiff, do they make eye contact with you or do they hunch their shoulders over a bit. There are several different signs that you can watch out for to determine what emotions the person is feeling, even if you are not able to get the information from the words that a person says. The signs to look for in nonverbal cues will include:

- Does the target move around or stand up straight? This is a sign that they are comfortable and open to talking with you. If you notice that there is too much movement going on, such as arm waving that is all over the place, and these movements are seen with a loud voice, then that person may be either excited or angry.
- If you notice that someone is using crossed arms, a quiet voice, and hunched shoulders, this usually means that they are nervous or uncomfortable. If they refuse to make any eye contact with you,

then this means they may be feeling a bit guilty about something or upset.

- Individual personalities, social situations, and even culture can influence the way that people will express their emotions through the body language. Facial expressions are often the most reliable with this because most countries use them in some form. Other nonverbal cues can be hard to translate into different cultures. For example, many Italians like to move their arms any time they speak, but in Japan, this is seen as impolite.

The next thing to notice is the other person's body movement and their posture. You should look at the entire body, in addition to the facial expressions we talked about before, to help you read and then interpret emotions. Body movement and posture will not only be able to reflect the emotions of the other person, but they can give you a good idea of how intense that emotion is.

Some of the different nonverbal signals you may notice include:

The Torso and the Shoulders

If you notice that someone is hunching their shoulders and then leaning forward a bit, this is associated with intense anger. If the other person is leaning backward a bit, this is more of a sign that they are experiencing some fear or panic. If that person is standing up straight and they have their head and shoulders up high, this is a sign of confidence. When the target hunches their shoulders a bit or they slump forward, then it is likely that they either feel nervous, feel bored, or they are looking to you to give them some sympathy that day.

Arms and Hands

The arms and hands can tell a whole story when it comes to the emotions of the other person. If your target is sad, they are more likely to place the arms near their sides and you will find the hands in their pockets. If that same target is irritated or annoyed about something, they will place one arm on the side or on the hips. They will then use the opposite hand for gesturing; making sure that their palm is flat. If that target is feeling indifferent, then both the hands will be found behind their back.

Legs and Feet

If you are looking at the other person and notice that they shake their legs or will go and tap the toes continuously, then this is a sign that they are in a hurry, annoyed, or a bit anxious. However, remember that sometimes this is just a nervous tick and it may mean nothing. If you notice that someone is doing this, but there are no other cues to show this, then it's not a big deal.

For most people though, you can look towards the legs and the feet to tell if someone is nervous. If the person is calm and collected, they will likely have their legs and feet pretty still. They won't move about from one foot to the other, but be planted pretty safely on the ground without a lot of movement during the conversation.

Another thing to look for is the signs of fight or flight in the person you talk with. When there is something unexpected that happens, whether it is a good thing or a bad thing, it is going to stimulate the brain in a way that you can't directly control. This is going to result in some physical responses like dilated pupils, more sweating, a faster heart rate, and rapid breathing

You should be able to tell if the person is stressed, anxious, or nervous by looking for some cues. These cues would include sweaty arms or palms, a face that is flushed, or hands that shake.

Men and women are going to show this stress in different ways. When a man is stressed out, they are more likely to show it through anger, aggression, and frustration. But when women are stressed, they may seek out help from their social group or become more talkative. There are also personalities that will become quiet and withdrawn any time they start to feel an emotion that is negative.

The easiest way for you to tell what emotion someone is feeling is to simply ask them. This method is direct, and if they are willing to tell you, then it can save a lot of time and hassle. Just keep in mind that sometimes the other person will lie or try to hide their feelings. If you take them at their word, then you will miss out on some important details about that person and how they are really doing.

If you want this method to work, the best option is to speak to them when you both can be alone, rather than around a lot of other people. Many times the target will be more truthful about the emotions they are feeling when they know the other person and when they don't feel like they have to share that emotion with a lot of other people.

Reading the emotions of another person doesn't have to be that complicated. You just need to learn how to read the different nonverbal cues that they send out. Most people don't even realize that these signals are going out, and this can really help you out because the target won't try to hide anything from you. As you work on increasing your emotional intelligence and looking for these nonverbal cues, you will find that it is easier than ever to tell the emotions that someone is feeling, even if they are not willing to directly tell you these feelings through their words during the conversation.

Chapter 2: How to Analyze People

Another aspect of emotional intelligence that you can work on is learning how to read people. Being perceptive about the feelings of other people, and being able to accurately guess their thoughts can be an important skill that can do wonders for helping you get through your interpersonal relationships. Though each person is going to be different, we are going to share some similarities in the way that we are wired. Being able to recognize some of these similarities can help us build better relationships and be there when others need us most.

Many times the biggest roadblock to your success is the ability to interact with other people. You may wonder what they are thinking about, how you can get along with them better, and what you may be missing when you talk to them. This is something that many people worry about, but they just don't know how to make it better.

You may have noticed that some individuals are able to get along with anyone. They can meet someone new and become best friends with them within five minutes. They know all the people that they need to talk to and meet in order to get ahead. And they never say the wrong thing, no matter what situation they are in. While others may be envious of these skills, this chapter is going to show you how to do this exact thing.

There isn't a magic eight ball that can tell you how to interact with other people. But if you know how to analyze them properly, you will find that this opens a new world of how to interact with each one. You will better be able to guess what they like to talk about, what makes them uncomfortable, and even know what emotions they are dealing with at that time. Let's take a look at some of the things that you can do to effectively read people, regardless of if you are best friends or you just met someone new.

Establish Your Baseline

To get started, you simply need to know the person. It is easier if you know them really well, but these ideas can be done on someone you just met. If you are just starting out with your emotional intelligence, then it may be best to try out some of the techniques on someone you have known for some time. When you get to know someone on more than just a superficial level, it is easier to know what they like and dislike, what they like to do on a regular basis, and what will constitute at a cue or a tell with them.

You should always base the opinions that you have about someone on two or more encounters with them. If you base this opinion on just one encounter with the person, you are going to miss out. People can speak or act differently based on the situation. You may have met someone when they were having a really bad day and everything was going wrong. Do you really want to base your whole relationship with that person because of that one day?

As you get more experience with this, start to pay attention to the habits that you see in others. Do you notice that they maintain eye contact with you at all times, or do they look away and have trouble with this? Do you notice that they get a change in their voices when they feel nervous? When that person is preoccupied, how do they let you know? These are just a few of the questions that you can ask to get a good read on someone.

You can also get a read on someone by asking questions that are open-ended. Any time that you are getting to know someone or reading them, you should spend the majority of that time watching and listening, rather than talking. Ask questions and then take a step back and enjoy what the other person tells you. Open-ended questions are the best because they require more than just a yes or no answer. This means that the other person will need to go into some details to actually answer the question. This reveals more information to you and can help keep the conversation going.

After you have had some time to establish a baseline, you can then look for if any inconsistencies show up in this baseline. If you know someone who is normally really affectionate, but one day they seem to not be present or they don't want to be near anyone else, then it usually means that something is going on. They may have received bad news, be having a bad day or something else is going on. Once you recognize this, you can ask questions and get to the bottom of the problem quickly.

Any time that something feels like it isn't adding up, you will need to ask that other person way. Perhaps that person is just tired, got in a fight with a family member, got in trouble at work, or they have some personal issues that are bothering them. Never just assume that the difference in personality or attitude is about your relationships because it most likely has something to do with other circumstances in their lives. If you know the baseline of that person, it is easier to catch when these things occur.

Always look for more than one cue to see if something is going on with someone. For example, if you are working with someone and notice that they lean away, it may have nothing to do with you and could simply be the chair is uncomfortable. If you notice that they are shaking their leg quite a bit, it could be a nervous tick that they always do.

You will want to take cues from three or four signs before you make any assumptions about the person. You can check out their face, their body, their tone of voice, and the words that they use. Once you have a signal from each of these sections, you can start to read the person and see if something is going on. You can also be more direct and just ask the person if needed.

And to end this section, you must know your own weaknesses. Everyone has weaknesses, even if they seem perfect to you. Knowing what your own weaknesses are can be so important. Don't ignore these weaknesses, they make you unique and can give you a unique picture to bring to the table when you meet new people, and when you are trying to read them.

Pay Attention to Any Body Language You See

We are going to spend some time talking about body language and why it is so important when you are trying to read someone or when you want to portray yourself in a certain way. Often, the body is going to speak more than the words the other person says. It can open up their inner thoughts, let you know their emotions, and can make it easier to tell what is going on with that person.

The first thing to look at when reading someone's body language is how they hold themselves. Right away, you should be able to tell how comfortable the other person feels around you. Sometimes how comfortable the person feels will have to do with you, it could be about some personal issue you don't know about, or it could be because they are not comfortable with the topic that is going on right then.

Some of the signals or language cues that you can look for when you want to tell if someone is comfortable or feeling positive include:

- Smiling. The smile shouldn't look like it is forced or through gritted teeth.
- Eye contact that seems natural
- Relaxed limbs that are placed comfortably at their sides.
- Leaning close to or into someone.

There are also some negative or uncomfortable body language cues that you will notice include:

- They have trouble maintaining eye contact and will often look away when they talk to you.
- The limbs will move around a lot. You will notice that they may do some nervous tapping of the leg or the fingers.
- Their legs and arms are crossed as if they want to protect themselves.
- They lean away from you.

You can also see if the other person will touch you. This will be where the baseline comes into play again. If the other person normally hugs you when you meet together, but then they don't one time, this means that they may feel some tension to you. Or if you notice that the other person has a handshake that is weak, it could signify that they are uncertain or nervous.

The body language of touching can sometimes be tough. Each person is going to have their own personal bubble, and simply because the person touches you a lot, doesn't mean that you are getting along with them. And if someone doesn't touch you a lot, that doesn't necessarily mean that you did anything wrong; they may just not like to touch those they are not familiar with.

The distance between you and the other person will matter as well. How far away or close the other person is from you will give you some great insight into what they are thinking. For example, if you notice that the other person seems to lean away from you or is distancing themselves from you physically, then they may not want to be intimate, maybe in a hurry, or they don't want to be vulnerable with you.

But a person who is willing to stand close to you will be more open and ready for a conversation. They may be happy or excited. They are often looking for friends to hang out with and want to share their stories or be involved in your own.

The Vocal Cues Can Make the Difference

The tone of voice that the other person uses is often more important than the words that actually come out of their mouths. How many times have you talked to someone who promises that they are fine, who tries to convince you that they are happy or excited, but something in the tone of their voice makes you question that completely?

The tone of voice that someone uses is going to tell you a lot about what that person is feeling. You want to listen to the tone to find out if there are any inconsistencies in the pitch or the tone. Is the person having trouble keeping a consistent voice, and they end up alternating between angry and happy? If this happens, then they may be trying to hide something from you. Some of the vocal cues you can look for include:

- Note the volume: Do you notice that the person is talking either quieter or louder than usual?
- Is the person hedging with their voice? Do they say words like "uh" or "um" often? This will happen when the person is buying time, lying or feeling nervous.
- See if the tone is conveying the same emotion that the words are. Is the person angry or sarcastic?

The length of a response can mean a lot too. Responses that are short and clipped could mean that this person is busy or frustrated. But if the person has some longer responses, it is a good sign that they are interested, or at least happy, with the topic of the conversation.

It is also good to look at the words that the person chooses to use. There are a lot of different ways to say the same thing, but they can all mean different things. When people tell you something, there is always going to be a process that underlies this content. If someone said something like "You're dating another dental hygienist?" you may be curious about the word "another" being present in what they are saying. They may be implying that your past dating history with a dental hygienist didn't go well, so why would you go through and do it again.

This can show up in many different ways. Using the term "yeah, no" is different than just telling the other person no when they request something. Adding in the word "dude" to something can show solidarity and shows that the two people are friends together. Looking at the words that the other person chooses to use can really help to show you what they think about a situation and what is going on in their heads.

How Can I Tell If Someone Is Lying to Me

There are many times in your life when you will need to be able to figure out whether or not someone is telling you the truth. This is a part of healthy relationships and you want to make sure that you can build up trust and more with the other person. But if they constantly lie to you, it is hard to feel like there is a connection.

If you know someone for a long time, it is easier to tell if they are lying to you. You already know their normal cues and body language and you will know when something seems off. The longer you know someone, the easier it is for you to see when someone is lying to you or not. But if you have just met someone, it may be harder to figure this out.

One of the most common reasons that people want to be able to read someone else is because they want to see if that other person is lying. When you are observing someone to see if they are lying to you, you will want to look for cues and body language that will correlate closely to them feeling nervous. You will need to look for more than one sign, but some of the signs that you need to focus on include:

- Check to see if there are any voice changes, or if there is all of a sudden a change in the body language they are using. For example, if your spouse is someone who likes to touch and hug you often, but then you ask them about something and they stop doing this, it is likely that they are lying.
- Do not mistake someone who looks to the side or who has trouble with eye contact for someone who lies. There actually isn't much of a relation between eye contact and lying. It is possible that they are lying, but it is just as possible that they are nervous or anxious.
- Check to see if the story you are being told is too elaborate and has too many details. Sometimes when someone lies, they are going to spend the time rehearsing what they will say beforehand. When a story sounds too good to be true, or like it has

been rehearsed, then this is a sign they are lying to you.
- If you notice that the person is fidgeting and moving around quite a bit, then this is a giveaway that they are lying to you.
- Look at the eyes of the other person. If the pupils start to grow bigger when they are talking to you, that part may be a lie.

Of course, any single one of these cues could be a sign of another emotion. But if you see a few of them put together, it is more likely that the other person is telling you a lie.

Being able to analyze the people around you can be a great skill to learn. It helps you to better understand the people you are trying to form relationships with. It helps you to get ahead at work or in your personal life. But you will need to take some time to practice these skills, maybe starting with the people you are close to before moving onto someone you just met, to help you get better at reading anyone near you.

Daniel James
Chapter 3: Persuasion Techniques

There are a lot of different persuasion techniques that you can use in order to convince someone to behave in a certain way. You will often have to almost trick them to get them to act in the way that you want, but it is often beneficial for both parties, so it is not as bad as manipulation.

We are often confronted with persuasion in its different forms each day. According to a study done by *Media Matters,* a typical adult is going to see at least 600 ads in various forms each day. Food makers want to get you to purchase their latest items, movie studios want you to see the latest movie, and clothing stores want you to purchase their new outfits and more. And these are just the forms of persuasion that you will see from advertising. Our friends and family can also try to persuade us as well.

Persuasion is not just something that salesmen and marketers will find useful. You can even learn how to work with these persuasion techniques in your own life in order to help you become a better negotiator and get what you want. This can be useful whether you are trying to get a raise at your job or if you want to convince your toddler to eat more of their vegetables.

Things to Know About Manipulation Before Starting

Because the two terms are similar, sometimes persuasion and manipulation are going to be used interchangeably. There are some differences though. With persuasion, you are not trying to be mean or force the other person to do something they don't want to do. Manipulation will be more like trickery to get the other person to behave in a certain way.

Before you can effectively use any of the persuasion techniques that are in this chapter, it is important to know some of the basics that come with persuasion. These include:

- Persuasion and manipulation are not the same: Manipulation is more like coercion with force in order to get the target to do something. The task that is done is not often in the interest of the target. On the other hand, persuasion is more of an art of getting people to do things that benefit both parties. Both you and the target will benefit from the interaction. If you sell a product, the target would benefit from having and using that product and you would benefit from making money off the sale.
- You can only persuade those who are persuadable. While it is true that anyone can be persuaded at the right time or context, it is hard to persuade everyone in a short amount of time. A good example

of this is that a lot of political campaigns are going to focus their money and time on just a few swing voters, the ones who decide elections, rather than on the whole country because they just don't have enough time to persuade everyone. This is why the first step you should take with persuasion is to identify those who are the most persuadable, in a short amount of time, to your point of view. Once you have this group, put your time and energy into persuading these people.

- The timing and the context: These two principles are the building blocks of persuasion. The context will create the standard of what is seen as acceptable. But timing is going to dictate what we will want from others and from life. A good example of timing is that we may choose to marry someone different than the type of person we dated when we are younger, simply because what we want during those two times has changed.

- The target has to be interested before they can be persuaded: You are never going to be able to persuade someone who has no interest in the product you are selling, or in what you are saying to purchase your product. If someone has an avid dislike of guns, you are never going to convince them to get a gun. Spend your time finding those who are going to be the most interested in the product you are selling or what you want to influence them with, and focus your energy there.

Since influence is useful in many aspects of our lives, no matter what we do, persuasion techniques are very useful as well. And many of these techniques have been studied and observed for many years. If you are interested in using some of these techniques in your own life to get what you want and to become a better negotiator, then here are a few tips to help you get started.

Some of the General Rules with Persuasion

- Reciprocity can compel the other person to fall under your influence: When I do some kind of favor for you, you are going to be compelled to do some other favor for me. This is a part of our DNA to be there and help out others. This means that you can leverage this process, and in some cases, use it to tilt the situation in your favor. When you provide some small gestures of consideration to others around you, it is easier to ask them for something back, even if it is bigger. And since you provided those gestures to them, they are more likely to agree to your request.

- Persistence will pay: The one who is the most willing to ask for what they want, even if they have to ask many times over, and the one who can keep demonstrating its value, is the one who will be considered the most persuasive. The way that other people have been successful in the past is because they stayed persistent over time with their message and any endeavor they undertook.

- When you give compliments, make sure they are sincere: You will be amazed at how much people respond to compliments. It makes them feel good and can form an instant connection between you and the other person. But you need to make sure that your compliments are sincere to help build that trust up. This can be a really easy thing to implement into your day. Try to compliment someone today, preferably for something they don't typically get a compliment about, and see what a difference it can make.

- Build up some rapport: It is a common human trait that we are going to like people who are like us. This is going to extend to many different parts of our lives. By matching and mirroring others in their habitual behaviors, you will be able to build up a sense of rapport where others will feel comfortable to you. And once that rapport is set up, the target will become more open to the suggestions you give.

Do I Need Any Personal Skills to Be More Persuasive?

There are some personal skills that can come in handy when you are trying to be more persuasive about your message. These help to create some more rapport between you and the other person and can make you the authority on the topic so that others trust you. Some of the personal skills that you may find useful when working on persuasion include:

- Being more flexible: When it comes to persuasion, you have to be a little bit flexible. Only offering one option to the other person, and not being willing to bend at all, can really ruin all the plans that you have. The one who is the most flexible during this time, and not necessarily the one who has the most power, will be the one who has the most control.

- Learn how to transfer your energy: Have you ever been around someone, or a group of people, who just seem to drain your energy out? You spend even five minutes with them, and you are tired, worn out, and depressed from all the work? On the other hand, have you ever been around someone who has a lot of energy and exuberance, and they are able to infuse you with it? The people who are considered the most persuasive are the ones who are able to take their own personal energy and transfer it over to others. This helps to motivate and invigorate each person. Sometimes this can be just a simple eye contact, and other times it can include active listening, excitement in any responses, laughter, and physical touch.

- Take the advantage with being prepared: Your starting point should always be to know more about the people and situations around you. being overly prepared can make you more persuasive to everyone you meet.

- If a conflict arises, learn how to detach yourself from that situation and stay calm: Sometimes you will talk to another person and you will have to handle it when they get heightened emotions. You will keep your leverage and advantage by staying unemotional, detached, and calm during that situation. In conflict, you will find that others turn to the person who is able to control their emotions, and they are more likely to trust these people. Be that person who remains calm and collected, and soon you will see how easy it is to get people to listen to you.

- Always be certain and confident: There is no quality that is more attractive to others than certainty. If you are able to have a lot of confidence and certainty, then you will have a much better chance of persuading others. If you really believe that what you are doing is good and will help others, you will find that it is not so tough to convince others to do what is best for them, while still getting what you want out of the situation.

- Use anger the right way: It is a well-known fact that most people are not going to feel comfortable with any conflict. If you are willing to take a situation and then heighten up the level of tension and conflict that is present, then it is likely the other person is going to back down. You don't want to do this when you are emotional or because you lose your control. If you use anger, remember that it needs to be used with a purpose to help you with persuasion.

Create a Need

If you want to be able to convince someone to do what you want is to convince them that they have a need that must be met. A very effective method of persuasion is to create a need or to appeal to a need that is already in existence. This technique for persuasion is going to work because it is able to appeal to the fundamental needs of humans for shelter, self-esteem, love, and self-actualizations.

Creating a need is a great method to use because once that need is created, then you are able to provide the solution that the person needs. Since you put that need in front of them and provide the solution that meets that need (and benefits you), then you can easily get someone to do what you want.

Appeal to a Social Need

Another method that you may want to use when you are working with persuasion is to appeal to the targets need to be similar to others, prestigious, and popular. Everyone wants to feel like they fit in with others, and if you are able to show the target that your product or your way is going to help them meet this need, and then you will be successful.

Television commercials are very effective at showing you this kind of persuasion. In these cases, the viewers are going to be encouraged to purchase one item or another in order to be like everyone else, to be well-respected, or to be well-known. Considering many Americans watch up to 2000 hours of television each year and see countless advertisements, and at this time, you can see how powerful this kind of persuasion can be.

Work with Words and Images That Are Loaded

Words and images that are loaded can be a technique that a lot of marketers and advertisers like to use. Marketers know that there is a lot of power that comes with positive words, and they try to use these as much as possible. This is why you will see words such as "all natural" and new and improved" on some of the products that you purchase.

Get That Foot in the Door

One popular technique to use with persuasion is known as the foot in the door technique. This one is going to work by asking a series of small requests out of the target in the hopes of getting them to agree since they already agreed to the request before.

For this one, you may ask the target to agree to complete a small request, like seeing if they will purchase a small item. Once the target agrees to that small request, you would then follow up this with a much larger request. Because you were able to get the person to agree to that small favor in the beginning, you already have your foot in the door. This seems to be able to get the individual to comply with the larger request that you give.

Let's look at an example of how this can work. You have a neighbor; you are asked if you are able to babysit their children for a few hours. You agree to help out and have a playdate between them and your own children. But after you agree to watch their children, the neighbor expands on this and asks if you are able to just keep the kids and watch them for the remainder of the day since you are already watching them.

Because you agreed to watch the kids already, you may feel that you are obligated to go with the larger request. And many times, this works and the neighbor would have you on the hook to watch the kids all day. Sometimes the target will be able to get out of it if they have something else going on at the time, but it can be very difficult to say no since you have already shown that you are willing to help the other person out.

Go Big Before Going Small

This is another approach that you can choose to go with, but remember that it is the opposite of what you see with the foot in the door technique that we discussed before. With this approach, you are going to start out by making a large request, one that is often realistic. Many times the person asking for this request knows that there is no way the target will agree to it, but they want that to be the starting point.

Since the request is so over the top and crazy, the target is naturally going to refuse it from the start. Instead of giving up, you will then respond by making a smaller request. This looks like you are trying to be conciliatory for that first, big request. Since you are acting sorry for such a big request, and the target feels bad that they had to turn down helping you, they may feel more obliged to take this second offer and help you out.

A good example of this is in sales. A salesperson may be in the business of selling vacations. The first offer may be for a big two-week cruise vacation that costs $10,000. The target, who has a much smaller budget than this and knows that they would never be able to take that much time off from work, will turn down the offer.

From here, the salesperson will retract that offer and then come in with a smaller offer. They may even ask the target some questions to make sure that the new offer is closer to the needs of the target. The second request maybe comes in at only $4000 for the vacation and lasts for five or six days instead. Even if this second offer is a bit more than what the target was wanting to spend, they are able to compare it to the first offer and see that the salesperson is trying to be more reasonable. The target will be more likely to purchase the second option because they feel compelled to do it.

Remember the Power of Reciprocity

Reciprocity can be one of your best friends when it comes to the idea of persuasion. It is the idea that you do a favor for someone else, so they will do a favor for you to pay you back. This one does require that you actively help someone out, but often the favor that you provide doesn't have to be huge in order to get the person to do a favor for you.

Many people feel a social obligation to do something for someone else simply because that other person did something for them. This is what is done in polite society, and you can easily use this to your advantage to get what you want. You will need to do the favor first, but then the other person will feel obligated to do a favor back for you to make it up.

Marketers can use this tendency to help sell a product. If they do a good job with it, they can even make it seem like they are doing you a kindness so that you accept their offer. A marketer may offer to put on some discounts or extras to the product, maybe saying they do it because you are such a great customer, and this can compel the person to take the offer and make a purchase.

You can also do this in your personal life. Say that you want to get someone to help you move some of your items in your home around because you can't do it on your own. As soon as you see an opportunity, you agree to help them out. Perhaps you would help them get a project done or you grab them lunch one day. Now that you helped them out, even though it wasn't the exact same thing that you needed, the other person will be more compelled and willing to help you out when you ask for your favor.

Disrupt Then Reframe

The next persuasion technique that you can use is the disrupt then reframe technique. The key here is to disrupt the intuitive thinking processes that most people have simply by playing with the words that you decide to use in your request.

An example of this would be changing "it's $3 for 8 cards" you would say something like "it's 300 pennies for 8 cards." You could change around words as well, such as changing the word cupcake over to halfcakes to help you to sell more baked goods in your store. Charities looking for donations have found some success changing words around, such as saying money some instead of some money.

However, disruption is only half the story with this one. Next, you need to work on reframing. This needs to happen right away, while the cognitive faculties of the other person are still disrupted. You may want to end your spiel with things like "it's fun!" "It's good for you" or "it's a bargain!" can all help to reframe the situation for your target.

With this part though, remember that reframing is only going to work within the moment that the target is distracted. If you are able to put the disruption first, this can help increase how susceptible the target is to the reframing statement that you choose and can reduce any excuses or counter arguments the target may try to use. And since you did the unexpected disruption, the brain will beg for this cognitive closure.

Legitimize Even the Smallest Favors

This is such a simple technique of persuasion, but many charities and other groups have found that it is really efficient. This is when you will make even the smallest amount of something (such as a donation, an amount of time, a favor or something else), sound useful and legitimate. You would use terms like "Even one second of your time would be fantastic" or "every little penny can help."

Just like with the disrupt then reframe technique from before; this one is going to work really well when you verbally talk to someone. And even having that kind of statement on a t-shirt, even if you don't say it out loud, has been effective in the past. For example, one study found that writing out the message "Even a donation one time in your life will help" on some t-shirts resulted in almost two times the number of people giving blood for the cause. And all that they changed was the simple writing on the shirt.

But why does this method work so well? Right now, psychological research doesn't have a good answer for why this works. It could simply be that compliance is less avoidable when just a minimal amount of help is needed. Since it only takes one time, or it only takes a second, or just a small donation is needed, it is harder to make excuses as to why you aren't willing to help.

It may also be that the technique is going to induce some shame or guilt on the other person, and this will jeopardize the helpful citizen image that the target wants to have. Or, it may have more to do with the fact that the request seems so desperate that it makes the target believe that the cause is so desperate to get help that anything is better than what they have.

But You Are Free Technique

The next technique that you can use for persuasion is one known as but you are free, or BYAF. This is a technique that was developed in France during 2000 and with 42 studies that had more than 22,000 total participants, this technique can double your chances of someone saying yes to your request.

The best thing about this is that the technique is so simple to use. The first step is to make your request. Then, at the end of the request, you will add in the line "but you are free". This shows the other person that they are the one to make the choice. The most important part of this is to recognize and talk about how the target has the freedom to say no to your request if they want to.

The exact way that you word this is not going to be so important. You will be able to get results from this one no matter which words you decide to use. You can use the "but you are free" or you can choose to use things like "but you don't have to" or "but obviously do not feel obliged".

In fact, there was a study published recently that found that just by wearing a shirt that had the word "liberty" on it when you make a request could induce the BYAF persuasion effect, even if you do not use those or similar words in your request. This technique is just so powerful!

Daniel James
An Anchor Point in the Negotiations Can Really Help

Having an anchoring point any time that you negotiate with someone can make a big difference. The anchoring bias is going to be a cognitive bias that is pretty subtle, but it will have a very powerful influence on decisions and negotiations. And if you learn how to use it properly, you can easily get the other person to do what you want, while they think that they are the one getting a good deal in the process.

When you are trying to decide on something, the first offer that is provided is going to be your anchoring point, whether you realize it or not. Any other offer that is given will be based off that anchoring point and you can determine if you are getting a good deal when you compare it to that first offer.

Many times you may try to negotiate a pay increase. If you are doing this with your boss, you want to be the first person in the room to suggest a number. That gives you the power to decide what the starting point will be. In this case, you want to list a number that is a bit high. While it is unlikely your boss will agree to that high number, it can definitely be used to influence how the negotiations go and in your favor. The employer will not want to offer something too low compared to your initial request, and you will likely get a higher raise than if you let the employer come up with the number first.

Don't Always Be Available When the Other Person Needs You

Another technique that you can choose to work with is the idea of scarcity. If you convince the other person that something is scarce, only available for a limited time, will only have a limited amount of the product, or that there is something else about the product that makes its availability limited, then the person is more likely to jump on it. Things, including you, will become more attractive any time that they are limited or scarce. When it comes to marketing and sales, people are much more likely to purchase something if they learn that the sale will end soon or that the item is the last one.

You can use this in several ways to benefit yourself. If you are in sales, you would use this idea to make the other person feel that their time is limited to get the product. You can say that there are only a few of this product left and that your company won't get any more. You can offer a sales price to the customer and tell them that it is only available for the weekend before the price goes up. This helps to build up scarcity for the other person and makes them more likely to purchase that product.

You can also use this in the world of dating. If you are always available, always texting someone new, and bothering them all the time, they may not be worried about losing you. They figure you are going to keep bothering them, so they have time to play the field a little bit and you will still be there. They may have gotten used to you being available any time they wanted to get together, but they are hard for you to get ahold of when you want.

Take a break from this, and limit when you are available. You don't need to be mean when you use this strategy, but instead of always agreeing to go out at the last minute when the other person wants to, you say that you have a prior engagement. When you are at work, don't answer the text message right away, but get to it when you have more time. The other person will start to realize how valuable you are and want to spend more time with you.

These are a few of the different persuasion techniques that you can employ to help you get what you want from other people. These are fairly simple techniques, but they can do a lot when it comes to helping you to persuade people to do something when you ask.

Chapter 4: Manipulation Techniques

All of us want to be able to get our needs met, but when it comes to a manipulator, they are going to use methods that are not often accepted by society and are kind of underhanded. Manipulation is a way to influence someone to act the way that you want with either abusive, deceptive, or indirect tactics. Sometimes the manipulation that is used is going to be friendly or kind. But this is because the manipulator has the skills to trick their target into thinking they will both benefit when in reality, only the manipulator is going to benefit.

In other instances, the manipulation is not going to be friendly or benign at all. In these cases, it can be abusive and veiled hostility. The objective in these scenarios can sometimes just be to gain power. It is possible that you wouldn't even realize that you are being intimidated by the manipulator.

The manipulator is going to have a ton of weapons that they like to use in order to get their targets to behave in a certain way. These could include denying, lying, comparing, feigning innocence or ignorance, guilt, foot in the door reversals, emotional blackmail, fake concern, mind games, flattery, sympathy, and apologies to name a few.

One of the most common methods that are used by a manipulator is the technique of guilt. They may say something like "after all I've done for you" in order to get you to do something for them. They may be chronically helpless or needy to get you to help them out. In some cases, they are going to negatively compare you to someone else to make you feel bad so that you will do what they want.

There are some manipulators who will deny conversations, agreements, or promises with their targets. Or they may start up a new argument and blame their target for something that person didn't do just to get the power and the sympathy. This approach can be used to benefit the manipulator in several ways such as to help them get out of an agreement, a promise, or a date.

Manipulators are often going to voice assumptions about your beliefs and intentions, and then they will react to these assumptions as if they were true. They will do this to help justify their own actions or feelings, all while denying whatever you try to say in that conversation. There are times when they will act like the two of you agreed on something or decided on something, even if you didn't, and when the target tries to object, they will just ignore it.

A common technique that a lot of manipulators will try to use is the foot in the door technique. This technique is when they will start out by asking for a small request. The target will agree to this small request. Then the manipulator will ask for something else, their real request. Because they did this, it is sometimes harder for the target to say no to helping out with the second thing, since they already said yes to the first one. If you do a reversal, it is going to turn the words that you said around to mean something that the target didn't really mean in that situation.

If the manipulator does use this technique and you try to object to the second request, the manipulator is able to turn around the tables so that they are now the party that is injured. This means that the whole situation has become about them and whatever their complaints are, and you are the one on the defensive in this scenario.

A manipulator can also work with emotional blackmail. This is a more abusive technique that will include a lot of methods including guilt, shame, threats, intimidation, and rage. To start, shaming is a method that a manipulator can use in order to create some self-doubt in their target and make that target feel insecure. Sometimes, that shame can be hidden inside of a compliment, which makes it even harder to fight back. For example, the manipulator may say something like "I'm surprised that you of all people would stoop to that!" when you do something that they don't like.

This is just one example. The manipulator could use some other classic ploys in order to frighten their targets with threats, accusations, dire warnings, and anger. Some of the things that the manipulator may say in these situations include "At your age, you'll never meet anyone else if you leave." They could also play the victim card and say something to their targets like "I'll die without you" to make the target feel bad

Any blackmailer is able to frighten you with anger in the hopes that you are able to sacrifice your own wants and needs. Sometimes this isn't going to work so the manipulator may suddenly try to switch themselves over to a much lighter mood. The target will then be so relieved that the manipulator is feeling better that they are more likely to agree to what the manipulator asks.

Manipulators are often seen to have higher levels in some aspects of emotional intelligence. To start, they are able to easily read their targets. They know the triggers of these people and will be able to push them to get what they want the most. This doesn't mean that they use the information the right way, though, but they do have a talent for being able to read others and know how the emotions of their targets work.

The manipulator will miss out on a few of the other factors that are important for emotional intelligence. They will not care as much about providing a mutually beneficial arrangement with the other party; they are only worried about how things will work out for them. They may be able to read others well and understand the emotions of others pretty well. But they won't understand how to control their own emotions and they will use those emotions against the target, rather than using them in a way to benefit both people. This is why most manipulators will score low on their emotional intelligence scores.

There are many different techniques that a manipulator is able to use in order to get their target to behave in a specific manner. Remember that not all of these are the best methods to use if you are working on your emotional intelligence because they require you to deceive someone else, and this can really damage the relationships that you want to form with your emotional intelligence. But it is still important to know some of these techniques. Some of the most common manipulation techniques include:

- Lying: Manipulators are often going to lie. Some of them will lie about almost everything that they can. The point of doing this is to confuse the victim and get them to feel off-center. Lying is a technique that a lot of manipulators will use, psychopaths, will use it even more often because they don't see the problem with lying.

- Leaving out parts of the story: This one is similar to lying, but instead of telling something that isn't true, the manipulator will purposely leave out important parts of the story. They do this to make sure that the victim is missing out on some part of the story and this puts them at a disadvantage.

- Lots of mood swings: Not knowing the mood that the other person will be in from one time to another can be another technique. Changing from happy one moment to angry the next few minutes can really upset the target and can make them feel like they are off balance.

- Devaluation and love-bombing: This is a technique that is found with a lot of narcissists. They will go in and charm their target until that person is hooked into thinking the manipulator is the best person ever. Then things will change and the target will be left alone or feeling low because the manipulator just drops them.

- Punishment: This would include various techniques like physical violence, the silent treatment, and constant nagging.

- Denial: Many manipulators are going to take control of a situation simply by denying anything that they are accused of. They may say that they don't remember the situation or that they were never the ones who did that thing.

- Spinning the truth: Many manipulators are going to twist around the facts in order to make it work for them. They may not technically say something that is a lie, but they lead you to believe something is a certain way to fit their needs.

- Minimizing: This technique is when a predator is going to downplay their actions. They will try to convince their target that the action wasn't as damaging or as important as the target makes them out to be. Often this also results in the blame getting put on the victim because they overreacted to the situation.

- Plays the victim: This is a technique that works if you want to play on the emotions and the empathy of the other person. The manipulator is going to turn things around to make themselves the victim. This helps them to get more compassion and sympathy from those around them. It is in human nature to help out those who are suffering and so this works in the favor of the manipulator.

- Moves the goal posts: This is when the manipulator will always change the rules to keep the target off track.

- Diversion: The manipulator will use diversion in order to keep the conversation away from their own acts. They may try to move the conversation on to a new topic any time their target tries to bring up the behavior at all.

- Sarcasm: When the manipulator is in public with their target, they will often employ sarcasm. The point of using this technique is that it is very effective at lowering the amount of self-esteem the victim has and can show others how strong and powerful the manipulator is at the same time.

- Guilt tripping: Everyone has employed guilt tripping as a means to get what they want. But a manipulator will do this on a regular basis for several reasons. They may use this technique against their target by saying that the target doesn't really care about them, that the target is selfish, or that the target has a really easy life. The whole point of using the guilt trip technique is that it helps the manipulator to keep the target anxious and confused about what is right and wrong.

- Flattery: This is when the manipulator is going to use praise or charm on the target. This helps the manipulator to gain the trust of the other person. Most people are pretty happy to receive the compliments from this technique, but this also helps them to lower their guard and gives the manipulator a lot of room to work on them.

- Playing the innocent card: Any time that the target tries to accuse the manipulator of doing something wrong, the manipulator is able to feign shock and confusion at all of that. Often the surprise is convincing enough that the victim can start to question their own judgment in the manner.

- Over the top aggression: Sometimes rage and aggression will be used, often in such high amounts that it is meant to shock the target into submission. Anger can be used, even if the manipulator is not feeling all that angry, in order to shut down further conversation on a topic the manipulator doesn't want to dwell on anymore. With this over the top anger, the victim is scared, but they now have to focus on keeping that anger under control, rather than on the original topic.

- Isolation: The manipulator will find that it is easier to keep their target under control if that person is isolated from others. They may isolate their targets from friends and family members who may try to shed light and truth on that situation.

Many times, manipulation techniques and the use of them can be a sign of low emotional intelligence. It may get you what you want, but often others are going to catch on to the technique pretty quickly, and then will want nothing to do with you at all. These techniques do not make it easy for you to make friends or form the meaningful relationships that are necessary when you are trying to improve your emotional intelligence.

Chapter 5: Body Language Techniques

How your emotions can be seen in body language

With some careful observation, you are going to see a lot of emotions from the nonverbal signs that someone is sending out to you. In fact, these emotions are going to show up more in the nonverbal cues than in the words that the other person is saying. These are indicators that can give you a good look into what the other person really means when you are talking with them. Some basic body language signs you will notice with the different emotions include:

Anger

Anger is often going to show up when the achievements of goals are frustrated and the person isn't in control the way that they want. Some of the signs that someone is angry include:

- An invasion of body space and leaning forward
- Clenched fists
- The teeth will be shown and there will be some snarling
- The neck and the face will look flush or red.

Nervousness, Anxiety, and Fear

Fear is going to occur any time the basic needs of the person are threatened. There are different levels of fear; sometimes it is just a mild anxiety all the way to blind terror. The signs that you notice are going to vary based on the type of fear that is present, but some of the signs of fear include:

- Fidgeting
- Defensive body language that could include a drawing in of the limbs and crossing the arms and hands.

- Sweating
- There will be some tension in the muscles.
- Voice tremors
- Speech errors
- The tones of speech the person uses will go up and done.
- Trembling lip
- Damp eyes
- Not looking directly at the other person when talking
- Dry mouth. You can see this by the person rubbing their throat, drinking water, or licking their lips.
- Pale face
- The person is in a cold sweat

Sadness

Sadness is often going to be a type of depressive state for the person. They are going to feel bad about something, may miss someone, or another reason is present why they feel sad. Some of the signs of sadness include:

- Tears
- A speech tone that is pretty flat
- A trembling lip and trouble talking without choking up
- Drooping of the body

Embarrassment

It is even possible to see signs of embarrassment when you are looking at the body language of the other person. Embarrassment is often caused by a feeling of guilt or when a transgression of values occurs. Some of the signs of embarrassment will include:

- A false smile, the person changing the topic, and lots of grimacing.
- The person is always looking down and away from others and they are not able to look them in the eye.
- The neck and the face seem to be flushed or red.

Surprise

The emotion of surprise is going to occur when something unexpected occurs to the other person. They may be able to handle it a little bit, but often this is an emotion that is hard to hide and you will be able to see the results of it pretty quickly. Some of the signs of surprise include:

- A backwards movement that is sudden
- An open mouth
- The eyes will get wide
- The eyebrows will become raised

Happiness

And of course, there are signals in the body language of each of us that shows happiness. Happiness is going to happen when the needs and the goals of the other person are met. Some of the signals to show that happiness is occurring include:

- A body language that is open and will invite anyone in.
- A big smile, one that takes up the whole face, even the eyes.
- The muscles of that person will be relaxed.

The Body Language of Someone Who Is Happy

All of us like to be around others who are happy. They are able to give off an energy that is contagious and hard to ignore. They can even make us feel better about ourselves. But how do we know when someone is feeling happy? Sometimes someone will say they are happy, but the words are not enough to give us that idea. Some of the things to look for in the body language of someone who is happy include:

- More energy: When someone is happy, they will have more energy, and this shows up in their body language. The person will move around a lot to show this.

- Straight back: A happy person is going to have a straighter back and good posture.
- Talks more, smiles and laughs: When a person is happy, everything can make them smile and laugh. And they are more likely to keep on talking when they feel happy. In fact, a happy person often initiates the conversation more than others.
- Open body language: Any time that someone is feeling happy, their body language will look more open and relaxed. It is not common for someone who is happy to cross their legs or fold up their arms so look for these signs.

How to Use Your Body Language to Show Anger

It is likely that you have seen someone get angry in the past. It didn't take you long to notice that they either weren't happy with the situation or they were becoming angry at the things that you say. Anger is a good emotion to practice with when you are learning to recognize body language cues because it has some really distinct ones that are easy to recognize.

Someone who is angry is going to have their eyebrows tilted towards the center of their face or both of the eyebrows will be flat and lowered. This is very distinct from some of the other emotions and this is one of those where you will be able to tell whether or not someone is angry just by how their eyebrows look. The eyes are a giveaway as well. The eyes are going to have a glare to them. Sometimes the person will squint their eyes and other times the eyebrows will be flat and the eyes are wide open.

The mouth is going to show some of the anger as well. When anger is present, the mouth is going to narrow the lips until they look like the person is biting the lips or holding them so tight they are no longer able to get any words out.

There are also other nonverbal signs to watch out for. The angry person may decide to physically shake their fingers at another person and they will likely keep their hands and arms far away from the body. You can see other body language cues such as punching objects, waving the arms, stomping. Some people just ball up when they are angry and want to be left alone.

The Signs of Impatience in Your Body Language

There are many reasons why someone may be impatient with you. The two most common reasons include:

- They are not really interested in what you have to say or what you are trying to offer. This could be because the information bores them, or because they are just too busy at that time, and they are trying to get you to hurry on your way.

- They have somewhere that they need to be and they don't want to spend their time hearing what you have to say or listen to the offer that you have for them.

When someone is impatient, they may have trouble keeping eye contact while you two are talking. Sometimes they will even turn the head a little bit while the conversation is going on and you may notice they almost talk out of the side of their mouth. The head of that person can sometimes nod away from you and can look like they are trying to escape from that situation.

The shoulders and the torso can show some impatience as well. For example, the other person could shift away from you a bit and face more towards the door, or they may slowly inch away from you if they have somewhere else to be. They will lean away from you and if they get really impatient, you will notice that the breathing patterns of that person are going to change and get much deeper than before.

Some of the common body language signs that you will notice in someone who is impatient include:

- The feet start to shift away from the other person
- The head and the arms of that person will start to get overly animated.
- The face will start to show a pout
- The other person will not stay as close to you as before.
- If you notice that there is some foot tapping going on, then know the other person is impatient.
- Sighs or really deep breaths.
- A loss or a complete lack of eye contact or the person is glaring at you.
- There are arm and hand rolls.

The Signs of Surprise in Your Body Language

Surprise is a unique emotion that can use a lot of different features in the face. This makes it an easier emotion to learn from the nonverbal cues of the other person.

First, the eyes and the eyebrows will open up when the person is surprised. The eyebrows will often go up, straight up for most people, while the eyes will get wide and follow those eyebrows as much as possible. The mouth will open up wide, maybe in an O shape or with a big smile depending on the type of surprise the person encounters.

Not only can you look at the mouth, eyebrows, and eyes of the other person to find out if they are exhibiting signs of surprise, you can also listen to the tone of the voice. Often those who are surprised will have a higher pitch to their voice tone compared to how they normally talk.

They may also be a little bit breathless after the surprise so you can look for that sign as well.

The hands and feet can also come into play with surprise. When someone is surprised, their hands will often lift up or they will go in front of the core to help protect the organs of the body. The feet could get a jolt when they are surprised and depending on what surprised the person, they could come off the ground, causing the person to jump.

The Signs of Sadness in the Body Language

When you are looking at someone and trying to figure out whether they are sad or not, there will be some distinct features that will help you figure this out. This is especially true with the face of the other person, so look near the eyes and the mouth to find this out.

To start, we are going to look at the eyes. When someone is sad, the eyes are going to droop from the top and when you look at their eyes, they will not have as much focus as they usually do. It is almost like you or the other person is not looking at anything in specific. They are there, but there isn't really a purpose about what they are looking at.

The mouth can show sadness as well. If you are looking at someone who is displaying the emotion of sadness, the mouth is going to be turned down and the corners will have a slight pull to them. It is likely that the lips will have a little bit of a pout to them and if the person is really sad or close to crying, there could be some twitching near the corners of the lips as well.

The emotion of sadness can be really strong and it is not uncommon for it to leak over into other nonverbal parts of body language as well. For example, it is common for people who feel sad to move slower than normal. They may have their arms folded in like they are trying to hold onto themselves or give themselves a hug. This person could also have a breath that is slower than what is normal and they frequently keep their gaze downwards.

How to Use Your Body Language to Show Fear

There may be times when you need to figure out if someone is feeling fearful about a situation. There are several nonverbal tells that people will show off and no matter how hard they try, a few of these signals will show up. The first place to view for signs of fear is the eyebrows. The eyebrows are going to move upwards and then move to the center of the nose in one movement. In many cases, you will see the eyebrows go up as much as possible when the person is scared. You can also look into the eyes to see if there is any fear. The eyelids near the eyes will move up as high as possible and the bottom eyelid is going to flatten out.

The mouth can show fear by the way that it moves too. You will see that the mouth pulls back the corners of the lips so they start going near the ears. You may see that the lips look flat.

The body language can be a factor as well, although each person will display fear in a different way. Some people will cry when they are scared, some will even get angry because of that fear and the lack of control they have. Many will choose to pull their hands and arms near the body as a sort of protective barrier.

How Lack of Confidence Shows up in Body Language

Many people suffer from issues of low confidence levels. They may worry about what others think about them or worry that they are not good enough to be in a group or around other people. This lack of confidence has likely been around that person for a long time, and it is a really hard mindset to abandon. Because of this, there are some signs that present themselves in the body language of someone who has low self-confidence.

When someone is suffering from low self-confidence, they will often walk around with their heads down and the chin is close to the chest. Often, this person will have trouble making any eye contact, and if they do, it is only for a brief time. The face can also show some signs of low confidence. The face may be pointed down with a little bit of a pout or pucker to it. This is not always the same for everyone though. Some people who are struggling with low confidence will have a scowl or a frown on their face as a form of protection against others.

You can find that even the shoulders of someone with low confidence will be different. These people will have their shoulders rolled in, and sometimes they will disguise this motion with folded arms. The body movements of these people will not be as fluid as they should. The speed of the walk can give away some clues as well. They will sometimes walk at a slower pace or will not have the right fluidity in their stride.

There are many different emotions that someone can feel in their lifetime, and while some of the nonverbal body language cues are going to be similar between these emotions, often the cues are unique enough that you can distinguish one from the other if you are really paying attention.

Knowing these different body language cues can really help you when working with other people. You will be able to look for these nonverbal cues to figure out exactly how someone is doing, rather than just taking them at their word for it. This allows you to ask deep questions to get the answers and provide help as needed to those people. Overall, being able to tell the emotions of the other person, even if that person doesn't come right out and tell you what emotions they are feeling, can help you to form stronger relationships and increase your emotional intelligence too.

Methods to Use to Get Body Language to Influence Those Around You

While it can really help to learn how to read the body language of those around you, there are times when you will want to use your own body language to influence that other person. When you can make your target feel more at ease around you, then they are more likely to do what you want. Think about it; if someone makes you feel uncomfortable or nervous, are you likely to help them out when they offer you a product or ask you for a favor. Or would you be more willing to do these things with someone you feel comfortable with?

Using the right body language can help you to convey power, confidence, and assertiveness. And when you can portray all of that to the other person, you are better able to influence your target. Remember though, they are only going to be persuaded if they also trust you. This means that it is equally important to use your body in ways that make the other people feel like they are connected with you, rather than dominated by you.

Since we know all the importance of body language and how well it will work to influence others, let's take a look at some of the ways that you can use your own body language effectively so that you become more influential and persuasive to those around you.

Start Out With a Smile

This sounds like a simple thing to do, but one of the best tools for you when it comes to body language is a smile. This can make you come off as approachable, confident, and warm, traits that are great for getting trust from others. People are more willing to listen to what you want to tell them if they like you, and a smile is a great way to build up this kind of relationship.

The next time you meet someone new, it is important that you smile in a genuine way. This means that not only should your face show a smile, but your eyes should be in it as well. If you are in a bad mood at the time, try to think of someone you love or a happy occasion to help you get that smile.

Match the Movements of the Other Person

When you have had some time to build up a good rapport with the other person, it is easier for you to get that other person to listen to you. You are even more likely to get them to understand the point of view that you present to them. If the rapport is really good, then the other person is going to quickly warm up to you and will be more than willing to support any ideas that you present to them.

So, how do you build up this rapport with someone else? Some people find that building up this rapport is hard. But as you work on increasing your emotional intelligence, you will get better at building up this rapport since you can read other people better and know what they enjoy and what they want to steer clear from.

People who are able to build up this rapport are able to do it simply by finding some common ground and similarities to connect them. A quick way to do this is with using your body. Try mimicking the movements of the other person can do wonders in getting them to feel connected to you. You need to do this in a subtle way. If the other person suspects that you are copying them, they are going to feel offended and feel annoyed in the process. But if you can do this just a little bit, without them catching on, the other person is going to feel some connection with you, and they won't be sure why.

You don't have to do much to make this work. If you see that they cross or uncross their legs, then do the same thing. When they pick up a pen and then pick up yours. If they put a hand on the table, try to do the same thing. Once you see that the other person is unconsciously copying what you are doing, then you know that they feel connected with you and now you are in a good position to influence them.

Nod

Another trick to try out if you would like to get others around you to say yes, then try to get them nodding their head in agreement before you are even asking them a question. If you make a small nod at someone, they will have an unconscious urge to nod right back

While you are talking with this person, start to do a little bit of nodding as they talk. This can be done to either confirm or agree with the statements they are making. Then, when you do the nod, you can make some of your own statements and see how the other person will start mimicking you and nodding back. Since the person is already nodding at this point, they are more likely to keep agreeing with you, even when you make your proposal. This works as long as the proposal you give them is not unreasonable.

Stand Up

If the other person is sitting down and you are standing up, you basically have the upper hand in the conversation. Standing up above someone is going to give the impression that you are more powerful and dominant compared to them, so they will want to capitulate to you. It is important that you are not completely standing over that person though or leaning in so much that they feel you are too close and start to feel uncomfortable. Doing this will be seen as bullying and you will lose all your ground in the negotiations.

But simply standing up near the other person, while they are sitting down, can do the trick. This will ensure that they feel that you are an authority on the subject and that they should look up to you, both figuratively and literally. You will be amazed at how much this simple little step can get the other person to agree with what you say.

You can even use this method over the phone. Even if that other person isn't able to see you, standing up gives you the feeling of power and of being more dominant. You will naturally communicate in a more assertive manner. The next time that you are on a phone call where you need to influence the other person and the outcome of that phone call, try standing up, and seeing what a difference it will make.

Lean In

The way that you lean your body can make a difference on how well you can influence other people. For example, simply tilting your body or your head to someone is a good way to show others that you are interested in them. This is a form of flattery that others are going to respond really well to.

Any time that you are able to make the other person feel like they are being listened to and like they are important, then you have won. They are more likely to agree with what you are saying or whatever you propose to them. If you notice that they are copying you and leaning in as well, then this is a good sign that the two of you have some good rapport going on.

You do need to be careful about this one though. You don't want to lean in so close to the other person that they feel like you are on top of them or that you are invading their personal space. If the other person starts to lean back or takes a step back, then you have shown that you do have some control in this situation and may have the upper hand.

However, this stepping back or leaning back could show that you have made the other person feel threatened a bit. As soon as the other person feels threatened, then you have lost them. They will not feel comfortable working with you at all and you will never convince them to get your product or follow your idea. Be close to the other person and lean in to show some familiarity, but don't be on top of them or use approaches that would make them feel like you are trying to be aggressive.

Point with the Feet

The way that your feet, and your whole body, point can be seen as either a positive or negative signal. If you point your feet towards something, then this is positive. When the feet are pointed towards the person you are talking to, it shows them that you are actually interested in them and what they have to say. It is the first step towards building trust. If you want to put yourself over the edge with impressing the other person and influencing them towards a specific course of action, then pointing your feet towards them can make this happen during the conversation.

Another trick to use with this one is when you want to end the conversation. If you need to be somewhere else or you are getting tired of the conversation, then you can influence the other person so they will stop the conversation. All you have to do is point your feet away from them. Try pointing your feet, and a little turn of the body, to the door, and you will be amazed at how quickly the other person will stop the conversation because it is now time to leave.

The Power of Your Position

Any time that you have a big need to show someone that you are the one in charge, you can use your body. We aren't trying to do this as a way to intimidate them, but as a way to show that we have authority in the conversation or the topic at hand. This can often get the target to trust us more and take our advice on things, and we can then influence them to act the way that we want.

To start with this one, you will need to stand so that your feet are a good distance apart and your hands are on the hips. This shows the other person that you wish to be in control, and it has the power to release some extra testosterone into the system.

While doing this, you want to be careful to not act too aggressive or dominant. This can make the other person feel like you are going to be a threat to them and this can ruin even your best efforts. The best method here is to assume this stance for just a few moments before the encounter. This helps you to get a boost in your confidence levels.

Then, when it is time to meet the target you wish to influence, you can go with a position that is a bit more open, keeping the arms at your sides. This is a good stance to use during the conversation because it will display your confidence and also your trustworthiness, putting you in a positive light with your target and making it easier to influence them. Remember that positive perceptions from your target can lead to better negotiations, the strong relationship you want, and all the influence you could desire.

Your body language is going to make all the difference when it comes to how well you are able to influence the other person. You want to give off the right type of message with your body language can make all the difference in whether the other person trusts you and if they will agree to what you are offering. Try some of these body language tips out the next time that you talk to someone, even if you are not trying to influence them at the time, and see if they make a difference in the rapport you have, the reception you get from the other person, and more.

Daniel James
Chapter 6: Mind Control Techniques

Mind control techniques are interesting because they are tools that help you communicate with yourself, to better understand the abilities that you have within, and to help you to learn the best way to use your strengths to improve yourself. These techniques, while often portrayed in a negative light in the media and on television and movies, can actually help you to gain more control over your emotions, guide your thoughts, and give you the self-control that is needed to make it through life.

The thing about these mind control techniques is that they can work to better train your mind to use all its potential to tackle any difficult situation that comes up. Being able to learn these techniques and then practice them on a regular basis can help you to enhance your own mental abilities. If you are successful, you will be able to effectively work, win people over, find the peace of mind you want, and overcome all difficulties that come your way.

Mind Control Techniques to do on Yourself

- Self-hypnosis: this is one of the most effective techniques that you can use for mind control. It is going to use autosuggestions and you can use to it help increase your own motivation, reduce stress, and get rid of any bad habits. The way to perform this technique is to motivate yourself towards a goal, get to a relaxed state of mind, concentrate your energy on a set target, and then direct yourself towards that. Sometimes just visualizing the realization of that goal can help. Creative visualizations are good to change that perception and they can generate a feeling of pleasure. You may want to look up a few different techniques to use that can help you do self-hypnosis whenever you need.

- Re-education: To re-educate yourself, you simply need to teach it to yourself again. When you use it in mind control, it is going to help you instill certain positive beliefs, helping you to get rid of some of the negative emotions that you may be feeling. This method is good when you need to break some of your bad habits or when you are trying to discourage yourself from doing something wrong.

- Memory inhibition: This technique is there to help inhibit the occurrence of certain memories. It is the ability for you to turn off your mind so you won't hold onto any information that is irrelevant. It can sometimes be used for those who want to cast out memories that they no longer want to hold onto, such as sad or painful ones.

- Psychotherapy: Psychotherapy is all about bringing out a new and positive change in you. You will be able to do this by changing your behavior and attitude. This method may include the help of a professional such as a psychologist or a counselor. They will be able to listen to the problems you are having and can lead you to the right solutions. This type of communication is effective because it leads to a change in your behavior and it can help you to get better control over your mind and your life.

- Behavior change: This type of program is going to include a variety of activities that are there to focus on the different things that influence behavior. These activities can help you to feel discouraged from bad habits or addictions including overeating, drug abuse, and drinking.

- Positive messages: Playing tapes and reading books that all contain positive messages can all go a long way in helping to influence your thinking. A positive self-talk can sometimes have similar effects. You need to hear a lot of words that are encouraging, and ones that carry a lot of positive emotion, in order to get this same effect on your mind.

- Brainwave entertainment: It is possible to alter the mental state of a person through a method known as brainwave entertainment. This technique is going to have pulses of sound or light fed to the brain through the eyes or ears. In response, the brain is going to produce some impulses that are synchronized with the frequency or the pattern of those signals.

- Music: If you are trying to use some mind control techniques on yourself, then you may want to consider working with music. The power of music is really great when you are trying to change your mental state. For example, how many times have you had a bad day and went home to turn something upbeat on? Did it seem to help lift up your mood? This is an example of how music can change your state of mind.

- Subliminal messages: These types of messages are going to communicate with the subconscious mind and sometimes, the conscious self may not even be able to recognize them. Sometimes they are used to help instill certain behavioral patterns or certain values in the individual on a subconscious level.

- Meditation: No book about emotional intelligence is complete without a look at meditation. Meditation is used in many cases to attain a different level of consciousness and to help people be more in control over their emotional state. It helps to lower anxiety and high blood pressure and can make the whole body relax. It can even help you to feel more positive and happy. In the same line, breathing exercises are great to control the mind and body. Taking in deep and cleansing breaths when you feel tense and out of control can go a long way in helping you to release some tension in the body and get that anxiety or anger back under control before you lose it all.

- Non-attachment: This is the state of overcoming your attachment to desire for people or things. It is not easy to get into this state. When attached to desires and feelings, it is hard to become content with the way we are. The idea of non-attachment is that it paves the way to a life that is fulfilled. Instead of trying to go through life-changing what you dislike, you should choose to keep away from it or ignore it so that you can have inner peace. The ability to keep yourself unmoved can be a sign of good mind control in you.

The method of mind control above that you choose to use will depend on your circumstances. Some people want to be able to just change a behavior about themselves, so they will go with that option. Others find that meditation can be very useful for calming them down and helping them to be more in control of their emotions. You can choose the method that works for you, or combine a few together to help you get in charge of your emotions and increase your emotional intelligence.

Other Techniques You or Someone Else Can Use on Others

Many times mind control techniques will be used by one person, the agent, to take control over the thoughts and emotions of another person, or their target. These are often thought to be dangerous to use because they take the willpower of the other person away. But using certain techniques from each one can help you to influence people better, and you don't even need to take away their free will. Some of the other mind control techniques that you or someone else can use on others include:

Brainwashing

Brainwashing, often known as thought reform in psychology, is going to be a topic that falls into the area of social influence. Of course, we already know that social influence happens all day every day thanks to peer pressure, advertisements, and more. It is a collection of ways in which people are able to change the behaviors, beliefs, and attitudes of those around them.

Brainwashing is known as a very severe form of social influence. It is going to bring together a few different mind control approaches in order to try and change the way that someone thinks.

And it is often done with the consent, and even against the will, of the target.

Because brainwashing is known to be a very invasive form of influence, it will require the target to be completely isolated and dependent on the subject. This is why most forms of brainwashing will happen in places like prison camps and cults. If the target is able to get any kind of outside influence, it is hard for the brainwasher to get the end results that they want. The target can keep leaving and getting positive reinforcement that goes against the brainwashing, and the whole experiment is a failure.

The agent, or the brainwasher, is going to have complete control over their target. This means that the agent is going to be in control of the bathroom, eating, sleep patterns and other basic human needs fulfillment. The target doesn't have any control and can only do those things when it works well with the agent, making them completely depending on the agent. The agent will then be able to systematically break down the identity of the target until that identity is broken. At that time, the agent is able to replace that old identity with a new one full of beliefs, attitudes, and behaviors that work in the current environment of the target.

While it is widely believed that brainwashing could happen with the right conditions, it is pretty improbable, and it is not as severe a form of influence as the media might like to try to make it sound. The agent needs to be able to get their target completely under their control and they will have to work on this for a long time. This doesn't make it a very efficient technique to work on compared to the others.

Some of the definitions of brainwashing will require that there is some kind of threat present that pushes the target towards losing their identity. However, there are plenty of instances of brainwashing, such as in extremist cults, that wouldn't fit under the brainwashing umbrella if that definition were used since they don't often use physical abuse against their recruits.

Another definition is going to rely on nonphysical coercion and control as an effective means of brainwashing. This means that the agent will work to assert their own influence. No matter which of these definitions are used, many believe that under the ideal conditions for brainwashing, the effects of the process take a long time, can only be done on a small group of people, and the new personality could just be short-term. They believe that the old identity of the target is not completely erased in the process, and is just hiding. When that new identity is no longer reinforced, then the old beliefs and attitude could return.

In the ideal settings, it is possible for brainwashing to occur. According to psychologist Robert Jay Lifting, who studied former prisoners from the Chinese war camps and the Korean

War, there are a set of steps that are involved in the whole process of brainwashing. These steps include:

- An assault on the identity of the target.
- Guilt
- Self-betrayal.
- Reaching that breaking point.
- The agent offering leniency
- Compulsion to confess.
- A channeling of the guilt to a new method that is approved of by the agent.
- Releasing of guilt
- Progress and harmony.
- The final confession that allows the person to go through a rebirth.

Each of these steps needs to take place in an environment that isolates the target. Otherwise, outside influences could turn them away from the new identity that the agent is trying to use. This means that normal social reference points will be taken away completely. In addition, there are often many mind clouding techniques that will be used, such as malnutrition and sleep deprivation that will be used to help out with this process. And finally, the agent will often have some threat present of physical harm, which can make it even harder for the target to think in an independent and critical way.

Hypnotism

Any time the word hypnosis comes up, there are a lot of different pictures that may come to your mind. You may think about the mysterious figure that is seen on television or on movies who will wave a pocket watch back and forth to get their target into a zombie-like state. Then, when that target is in the hypnotized state, they will need to obey the hypnotist, no matter what the request may be from the hypnotist.

While this makes for some good material in books and in the movies, this representation doesn't really resemble what happens with real hypnotism. In fact, the modern understanding of how hypnosis works is going to contradict this concept through several points. The targets who are in this hypnotic trance are not going to be slaves to the hypnotist. They will still have their free will. In addition, they aren't really semi-asleep like most people think. In fact, these targets are going to be hyper-attentive.

The modern understanding of hypnosis has changed quite a bit, but there are still a lot of people who are confused about how it works and what it all means. Let's start with a definition of hypnosis and explore some of the different ways that it works, some of the techniques, and more.

Psychiatrists do have a good idea of the general characteristics that come with hypnosis, and they also have a model of how this can work. To keep it simple, hypnosis is a trace state that is characterized by relaxation, a heightened imagination, and extreme suggestibility. It is not really like the target is asleep, because that target will be alert and awake the whole time. It is more like the person is daydreaming or the feeling you get when you lose yourself in a book or a movie. You are conscious and alert, but you are able to tune out the other stimuli around you. You instead choose to focus all your energy on the subject at hand, while excluding everything else.

One school of thought concerning hypnosis is that it allows you to access the subconscious mind of the target directly. Normally you are only going to be aware of what is going on in the conscious mind. You will use that part of the mind to think about the words that you will say to someone, what problems are going on in front of you, and even when you try to remember where you place the keys.

But when you do these simple tasks, your conscious mind is working along with the subconscious mind, the part that is working behind the scenes. Your subconscious mind is able to access the reservoir of information that you need in order to do these tasks. It can even put together plans and ideas before running them by the conscious part of the mind. So, any time you have an idea that seems to come to you "out of the blue" this is because it was thought through with the subconscious mind. The subconscious mind is the one that will do most of the thinking for you and can decide a lot of the actions that you will take.

Psychiatrists think that the focusing exercises and deep relaxation of hypnotism will work to help subdue and calm down that conscious mind, forcing it to take a less active role when it comes to thinking. When you are in this state, you will have some awareness of what is going on, but the conscious mind has to take a backseat so the subconscious mind can get to work. This allows you and the hypnotist to work with that subconscious mind, without having to worry about any interference from the conscious mind.

If someone is trying to manipulate you, it is possible that they will try to use some of the techniques of hypnotism on you. They may not be able to put you in a full-on trance (they can't hypnotize anyone who doesn't want to be hypnotized), but they could work to relax the subconscious a bit so that you are more open to various suggestions that you hear.

There are a variety of methods that are available for a hypnotist to use on their target. There are also a few basic prerequisites before the hypnotist can be successful including:

- The target needs to be willing to be hypnotized.
- The target must have the belief that they can be hypnotized.
- The target must be able to get comfortable and relaxed at some point.

If these three criteria are all met, then the hypnotist is able to guide that target into a hypnotic trance. There are different methods that can be used, but some of the most common ones include:

- Eye fixation: This is similar to the method that we are familiar with in movies. The idea here is that the subject will focus all their energy on that object so that they can tune out the other types of stimuli that are there. As the subject focuses, the hypnotist will talk to them in a low tone in order to get the target to relax. This method is not used as much any longer because it isn't effective on most of the population.
- Rapid: The idea of working with this method is to try and overload the mind with some firm and sudden commands. When the commands are forceful and the hypnotist can be convincing enough, then the subject is going to surrender their conscious control over that situation. This is a method that works well for those who are doing stage shows because the

hypnotist can do this and put the audience on edge, so they are more susceptible to the commands.
- Progressive relaxation and imagery: This is the method that most psychiatrists are going to use. The hypnotist will speak to the target in a soothing and slow voice in order to bring about some focus and relaxation until the target has reached full hypnosis.
- Loss of balance: This method is responsible for creating a loss of equilibrium. It will do this with a slow and rhythmic rocking.

Many skeptics of hypnosis believe that the targets are not actually falling into a trance state. They believe that the influence of the hypnotist and social pressure are the leading force to convince someone that they should react in a certain way or do certain actions. Then, when the target finds that they are heeding the suggestions, they assume that they are in a hypnotic trance.

Those who believe this theory contends that this kind of belief is enough to bring about some remarkable changes in the person. For example, they think that if someone is compelling the target to act in a certain way, then that target is more likely to act that way. If the target thinks that hypnotic suggestion is the way to ease their pain, then the mind is able to bring this feeling about.

This can bring about an interesting point in terms of mind manipulation. The other person doesn't necessarily have to be in a trance to get these suggestions. They just need to believe the hypnotist and believe the actions that the hypnotist states. And then they will react in a certain way. The manipulator may be able to convince someone to react in a certain way because of their authority, their tone of voice, and more.

Propaganda

Propaganda is any information that is not considered objective and is used in order to further an agenda or influence an audience. It is able to do this by presenting facts in a certain way or omitting certain facts, in order to get the audience to react in a certain way. While there are different types of propaganda to watch out for, it is often associated with materials that the government would disperse. It can also come from the media, various businesses, and activist groups.

There are many different types of materials and media that can be used in order to get the propaganda message out. As new technologies are developed, there are more outlets for this. You may see this type of message being dispersed through websites, TV shows, radio shows, films, posters, cartoons, and even through paintings.

Propaganda is often developed to be highly inflammatory in order to get people fired up about a topic. If the government wants to get a new bill passed, for example, they may use propaganda in order to fire people up about the negatives if that bill isn't passed. They will paint the other side as the bad guy and will really highlight the negatives of not having that bill. And of course, they will conveniently forget all about the negatives of their plan or the positives of the other plan.

While propaganda can be used to get everyone on the same page and working together, it is often dangerous because of the reasons behind it and the information that is left out. Consumers and individuals who are not careful about the messages they read may be taken in with this mind control technique.

Chapter 7: NLP Methods

Neuro-Linguistic Programming, or NLP, is a set of skills that can reveal the kinds of communication that matter the most, on the inside and out. Let's break down some of the words in this process to help you understand more about what this all means:

- Neuro: This word refers to the mind, or the brain. In particular, it is going to refer to how the different states of the body and the mind will affect communication and behavior. NLP is going to teach more of a structural way of viewing these states, helping you to develop mental maps that show how things happen and how you can change the course.
- Linguistic: This word is going to refer to how these different states of the body and mind will be revealed, either through the words we speak or our nonverbal communication. Language is a major tool

that humans use in order to gain access to how the mind is working. NLP language patterns can sometimes teach us how to access information that remains in the unconscious and would be unknowable and vague without these techniques.

- Programming: This is going to refer to the capacity of the person to change their mind or their body state. Think about the term living on autopilot. For those trained in NLP, this means that you are just following your programming of habitual thoughts, reactions, feelings, traditions, and beliefs. Someone trained in NLP will know how these programs work in the mind and they are able to access them through basic conversation to help get these outdated programs and autopilot behaviors changed.

So, how does the idea of NLP work in the real world? When we are having a conversation with someone, many times it is easy to fixate on the words that the person is saying. You will concentrate on what the other person means and then your own rely as well. However, it has been known for many years now that the actual words people say are the least meaningful part of communication because they only convey about seven percent of what the other person means.

Think about having a conversation with someone who says they are willing to help you put together a social gathering. The words tell you, yes, but their facial expressions are bored or anxious and their voice is flat. The nonverbal communication is likely telling you that they really have no want to help out with the event, but they had offered just to be nice.

NLP is a system that helps you to better understand the majority of the conversation, all that nonverbal communication that says a lot without using any words. If you are able to master nonverbal communication, both your own and someone else's, then you will be a master communicator.

What is interesting here is that most people have no idea that there is so much to communication, more than just the words that someone says. There is an entire world of communication that occurs within your body and your mind. The inner life, such as your feelings, your attitude, and your mindset, is an active form of communication.

The Pillars of NLP

There are four foundations, or pillars, that come with NLP. These foundations include:

- Rapport: NLP provides you with a great gift to build up relationships with other people. Rapport is basically the ability to connect with others quickly. Creating this rapport means that you can create some trust with others. The way to build up this rapport is through understanding modality preferences, eye accessing cues, and predicates.

- Outcome thinking: An outcome is like your goal to get something done. The outcome is going to connect to thinking about what you want, rather than letting yourself get stuck in a more negative mode of thinking. Often the principles that come with this approach can help you come up with some good choices and decisions.
- Sensory awareness: NLP has the power to help you notice that your world is much richer when you start to pay attention to your senses, rather than just letting things happen around you.
- Behavioral flexibility: This means that you have the ability to do something different if the current method is not working. Being flexible is a huge part of NLP. It helps you to find some new perspectives and then build these into your day.

Anchoring

The first NLP technique you can utilize is anchoring. This is a technique that you would use to induce a certain frame of mind or an emotion in the other person, such as relaxation or happiness. This technique is going to use a word a gesture or a touch as an anchor that is the bookmark for the specific emotion and then that same thing can be used later on as the same anchor.

To understand how this works a bit better, try to remember a time when you were really happy. It can be any kind of memory that you would like, as long as the feelings of happiness are very strong. Now tell a story about that memory in your head, describing all the details as much as possible. Picture that moment in your head and then recall all the happy feelings that came with it.

At the same time, you can hold the index and the middle fingers on the right hand and give the fingers two quick squeezes. As you are completing the second squeeze, work to make the mental picture of that happy moment larger, bringing it closer to you, and imagine that the happy feeling is getting stronger. Now describe how you are feeling, what you were thinking when the situation happened. As you do this, squeeze the fingers twice. On the second finger squeeze, the feelings of happiness should double again. The more clearly you can imagine the feeling, the better this technique is going to work.

You will want to repeat these steps until you have been able to double the intensity of that happiness feeling at least five times in a row. This is the first part of the process. You are laying the anchor down at this time. Later you will be able to recall this anchor by using the same double squeeze to help recall that happiness.

In the mind, you are associating the neural signal of the two squeezes with being happy. This means that the more you lay down the anchor, and the clearer the feeling is, the better you can get this technique to work. You can also combine this with a few of the other NLP techniques that we will discuss later, in order to make the feeling as clear and vivid as possible.

A good example of how this works is the experiment by Ivan Pavlov. In this experiment, a bell was ringed each time the dogs were fed. The dogs soon began to associate the experience of eating time with the bell sound. Later on, the dogs would start to salivate just by hearing the ringing of the bell. This is the similar idea to what you are trying to do with the anchoring technique.

So, when are the times when you would use NLP anchoring? Anchoring is most commonly used in the art of seduction. The best example of this is when one of the parties asks the other about a happy memory they had in the past. When the seductee is "in the memory" or when they are laughing and smiling and having a good time, the person using seduction would then use a light touch or a distinct gesture to be the anchor. Whatever the chosen anchor is, you don't want it to be too obvious. If you make it too obvious, it is going to see out of the ordinary and the effect fails.

At a later time, the person using seduction will then be able to use their anchor in order to make their target feel the same kind of happiness that they did before. The target will start to experience that happy feeling again, but will start to associate those feelings with being close to the other person, and less with the happy memory. This may seem to be a bit of a swindle and like you are manipulating someone, but it is important to note that this anchoring technique in terms of seduction won't really be successful without some attraction between the parties to start with.

Pattern Interruption

Pattern interruption is a technique that is used in order to store keywords in the unconscious mind of your listener. This is sometimes combined with anchoring to give someone a message that appears to be heartfelt and signification. The way that pattern interruption will work is that it lures the inner monologue of the listener into a sequence or a pattern. Once this pattern has been established, you can then jolt them right out of the patterns at the critical moment before that pattern finishes. What this does is leaves the mind waiting for the next part of the pattern to happen, while their conscious mind will be distracted.

At first, this may seem confusing so we are going to work with an analogy. Let's say that you had an old man who has a dog that is able to do all the actions for him. The old man will be like our conscious mind and the dog will be the unconscious mind. The man will make all the decisions and the dog will perform the different actions that the man needs to be done.

With this idea, we are going to ask that old man to make us a sandwich. The man would then ask his dog to go into the kitchen and get some bread, some cheese, and some meat and then bring it out on a plate to you.

For the second step, we are going to again ask that man for a sandwich. The man would give the same commands as before. The dog would get the bread, the cheese, and the meat and put it on a plate and then SLAP! We now stop the sequence by slapping the man in the face and asking him to do a dance. Before the dog was given the final command of bringing the sandwich over, the pattern was interrupted and a new command was given.

The old man, the conscious mind is not as clever as the dog, or the conscious mind is not as clever as the unconscious mind, and he forgot about that final stage of bringing the sandwich. But the dog didn't forget about it. The dog may not be able to speak, but they are thinking what about that final command, I haven't done it yet. The dog will keep on thinking about this final command for some time.

You can take one more step here. If you are mean, you could also ask the old man to hand over his wallet. The man would ask the dog something like "hey dog, I'm thinking about giving you a command to bring me my wallet. I'm not sure, is 'bring it to me' something that you are used to doing?" Since you never finished the final command for the sandwich earlier, the dog would say something like "well yes, I've been waiting for a command like this one." And then it will bring out the wallet.

While this is not an exact example of what might happen with the pattern interruption, it at least gives us an idea of how it goes. This technique is sometimes a hard one to work with and accomplish, but if you are successful, you may see some great results in the process. It can be potent, especially if you add it in with some of the other NLP techniques.

Framing

Framing is an interesting technique because it is one that can often be used with some of the other techniques at the same time. The framing technique is more of an emotional de-amplifier or amplifier that will work by rebuilding or correcting the links that are currently present in your limbic system and which reside between the hippocampus and the amygdala.

The reason that the framing technique is so effective is that it is so simple and it can easily be used along with some of the other techniques that you choose to work with. Before we get too into that, let's take a look at some of the applications of framing to help it make a bit more sense.

In our lives, we learn a lot of lessons. Sometimes these come from good memories and sometimes they come from bad memories. While we may consider memories as good or bad based on the situation that surrounds them, in reality, the memories that you have are going to be highlight reels of events that happen in the past, and they are basically without any emotions.

To continue on, recall a memory that you have some negative emotions attached to. It doesn't need to be too traumatic, aim for something like an interview that didn't go well or failing a test. Once you have one, it is time to read on.

Without getting too technical about this part, the prefrontal cortex and your thalamus interacted together with the hippocampus and the limbic system to help you find the right memory to use. The hippocampus, which is the part of the brain responsible for storage and retrieval of long-term memories, has brought a picture up for you. It may include some small video snippets, a few sounds, but mostly the picture.

The amygdala, which is the part responsible for your emotions, will get to work. The memory is judged fresh, memories of emotions contained within that memory are going to be judged and then everything is linked to the amygdala, where you can then receive a short reminder of these emotions. With this particular memory, the emotions are going to be negative. But since the emotions are not stored with the memory, rather they are referenced when you bring out the memory, then it is possible for you to edit the emotions that your brain has associated with the memory.

This is where the framing technique can come into play. Framing is able to edit the emotional response that you have to a memory. To do this, we are going to bring out a memory of a bad interview, the one that you tried hard for but nothing went right with the whole thing. You can pick any memory that you want as well.

The first step here is to take the memory and then reduce the highlight reel that you have to just one snapshot that can help represent that memory. From here, you will want to take a step back from that memory. If you see the memory through your own eyes, then take that step back so you are able to see yourself in the situation. If you are seeing the memory in third person, then just go a bit further back to see more of the room.

Now that you are in the picture, make sure that you get a snapshot of that as well. Turn the picture into black or white and then make it a bit blurry or so it isn't in focus like it is an old photo. If you are able to, consider making it sepia in tone to give that older feel.

Put a frame on it, any frame that you would like, before hanging that frame and the picture on a wall. The wall can be anywhere that you like. Try out different lighting on the painting, watch other people look at the painting and then walk on from the memory.

At this point, as yourself how the situation feels. Does it still feel stressful or sad or anything else that is negative. This process should help you to notice a lessening of those feelings. Try this again, repeating the steps that we just did, and this will reduce the effect.

While this is a pretty basic example, you are using this exercise to help the mind take that memory and treat it more like a picture. This detaches the emotions from the memory and can trick the brain into dampening out any of the links to the emotions that this memory is able to refer to.

You can even try this out on someone else. You just need to read out the steps that you saw above to the other person. And when it is done, you can ask them how they now feel about that emotion.

Mirroring

The next type of NLP technique we will explore is mirroring. This is one of the most useful techniques you will use. If someone is good at the mirroring technique, then it is hard to dislike them, even when you find out what they are doing. Mirroring will simply be the process of mimicking some of the subtle and small behaviors that are present in the other person we are communicating with. This doesn't mean that you go start up a conversation with someone and copy every word they say back at them. This will annoy them and you won't build up any rapport with them. Mirroring needs to be subtle in order to work.

There are a few different things that you can do in order to achieve a mirroring of the other person. These include:

- The tempo, pace, pitch, tone, and volume of the other person.
- The specific choice of words or the vocabulary style of the other person.
- The body language and how comfortable the other person appears to be.
- Speech patterns that you notice in the other person.

Some people think that it is possible to mirror an accent of the other person. This one is a bit harder to do if you're not naturally inclined towards that accent over another. If you don't normally have an accent and then you start to mimic it, then that other person is going to notice, and this could make them feel like something is off, or you are making fun of them, and they won't want to talk with you any longer.

Mirroring can be a very useful tool, no matter who uses it. Take, for example, a waiter who relies on tips to help fill in their income. There was one study that worked with a group of waiters. The first group was told to use positive reinforcement with their customers. They would be positive with the other person, smile, say things like "great, sure, and no problem" when asked to do things, and so on. Then the second group of waiters was told to mirror the customers and they did this simply by repeating the orders back to the customer.

The interesting results here were that the waiters who used the mirroring techniques ended up getting a much larger average tip compared to the first group of waiters who relied on positive reinforcement. In fact, the mirroring technique let to a seventy percent larger average tip!

Mirroring can work well because it helps the other person feel more comfortable around you. Someone who is good at the mirroring process knows how to do it at a subtle level so it isn't easy to notice and no one gets offended. But when it is done properly, the other person can feel more at ease, a rapport can be built, and a new relationship can form in no time.

Conclusion

Thank for making it through to the end of *Practical Guide to Emotional Intelligence Mastery 2.0*, let's hope it was informative and able to provide you with all of the tools you need to achieve your goals whatever they may be.

The next step is to put a few of these techniques to good use. There are many times in our lives when we will want to influence those around us. The situations are not always mean or sinister. If you want to sell a product, get your boss to let you have a higher position or a raise, or when you want to ask someone out on a date, you could use some of these techniques for influencing to get them to do what you want.

This guidebook provided you with some of the techniques that you need to put your emotional intelligence to work and get the influence that you want. Whether you need to use manipulation, NLP, body language, or persuasion, you are sure to find the technique that works the best for you and what you wish to accomplish.

When you are trying to improve your emotional intelligence and you want to take it to the next level and really start to influence those around you, make sure to check out this guidebook to learn how it is done.

Finally, if you found this book useful in any way, a review on Amazon is always appreciated!

www.ingramcontent.com/pod-product-compliance
Lightning Source LLC
Chambersburg PA
CBHW030115100526
44591CB00009B/409